Conte

G000068907

IRELAND THE SONGS VOLUME 2

ISBN 1 85720 060 8

Copyright © 1993 **Walton Manufacturing Ltd.**
Unit 6a Rosemount Park Drive, Rosemount Business Park,
Ballycoolin Road, Dublin 11. Ireland.
US Distributors: The James Import Company. P.O. Box 874, New York, NY 10009, USA.

Printed in Ireland by Betaprint, Dublin

Priests crossing stream, Rostrevor, Co. Down. 1931.

Sally Gardens

The lyrics to this song were written by W.B. Yeats in 1889.

In a field down by the river my love and I did stand
And on my leaning shoulder, she laid her snow-white hand
She bid me take life easy, as the grass grows on the weirs
But I was young and foolish, and now am full of tears.

(Repeat first verse)

Deep in the Canadian Woods

There are not too many songs about the Irish emigrants to Canada but here is a rousing one by T.D. Sullivan written in 1857.

Deep in Can - ad - i - an woods we've met from one bright is - land flown__. Great is the land we tread but yet our hearts are with our own___. And ere we leave this shan - ty small, while fades the aut - umn day___, we,ll toast old Ire - land dear old Ire - land, Ire - land boys hur - rah!___ Ire - land boys hur - rah!___ Ire - land boys hur - rah!___ We'll toast old Ire - land, dear old Ire - land, Ire - land boys hur - rah!___

We've heard her faults a hundred times,
The new ones and the old,
In songs and sermons, rants and rhymes,
Enlarged some fifty-fold.
But take them all, the great and small,
And this we've got to say:
Here's dear old Ireland ! good old Ireland !
Ireland, boys Hurrah !

We know that brave and good men tried,
To snap her rusty chain,
That patriots suffered, martyrs died,
And all, it's said, in vain:
But no, boy, no ! a glance will show
How far they've won their way
Here's good old Ireland ! loved old Ireland !
Ireland, boys, Hurrah !

We've seen the wedding and the wake,
The patron and the fair,
And lithe young frames at the dear old games
In the kindly Irish air,
And the loud "Hurrah," we have heard it too,
And a thundering "Clear the way !"
Here's gay old Ireland ! dear old Ireland !
Ireland, boys, Hurrah !

And well we know in cool grey eyes,
When the hard day's work is o'er,
How soft and sweet are the words that greet,
The friends who meet once more:
With "Mary Machree!" and "My Pat, 'tis he !"
And "My own heart night and day!"
Ah, fond old Ireland ! dear old Ireland !
Ireland, boys, Hurrah !

And happy and bright are the groups that pass
From their peaceful homes, for miles
O'er fields and roads, and hills, to Mass,
When Sunday morning smiles !
And deep the zeal their true hearts feel
When low they kneel and pray.
O, dear old Ireland ! blest old Ireland !
Ireland, boys, Hurrah !

But deep in Canadian woods, we've met,
And we never may see again
The dear old isle where our hearts are set
And our first fond hopes remain !
But come, fill up another cup
and with every sup let's say:
"Here's loved old Ireland ! good old Ireland !
Ireland, boys, Hurrah !"

"Look at my toes!" Little girl in Kilkenny, 1925.

The Rose of Mooncoin

Seamus Kavanagh is the writer of this song and Mooncoin is a village in Kilkenny. It has become the anthem of the county.

How sweet 'tis to roam by the sun-ny Suir stream, And hear the dove coo 'neath the morn-ing sun-beam, Where the thrush and the ro-bin their sweet notes en-twine, On the banks of the Suir that flows down by Moon-coin.

Chorus

Flow on love-ly ri-ver flow gent-ly a-long. By your wa-ters so sweet sounds the lark's me-rry song. On your green banks I'll wan-der, where first I did join, With you love-ly Mol-ly the Rose of Moon-coin.

Oh Molly, dear Molly, it breaks my fond heart
To know that we two forever must part.
I'll think of you Molly, while sun and moon shine,
On the banks of the Suir that flows down by Mooncoin.
(CHORUS)

She has sailed far away o'er the dark rolling foam
Far away from the hills of her dear Irish home.
Where the fisherman sports with his small boat and line.
On the banks of the Suir that flows down by Mooncoin.
(CHORUS)

Then here's to the Suir with its valleys so fair
As oft times we wandered in the cool morning air
Where the roses are blooming and lilies entwine
On the banks of the Suir that flows down by Mooncoin.
(CHORUS)

The Leaving of Liverpool

Probably better known in Ireland than in Liverpool
this is a typical 19th century sea-song.

Fare - well to you my own true love, I am go - ing far far a - way.___ I am bound for Ca - li - for - ni -a. And I know that I'll re - turn some day.___ So fare thee well my own true love, and when I re - turn u - ni - ted we will be.___ It's not the lea - ving of Li - ver - pool that grieves___ me, but my dar - ling when I think of thee.___

I have shipped on a Yankee sailing ship,
Davy Crocket is her name,
And Burgess is the captain of her
And they say she is a floating hell.
(CHORUS)

Oh the sun is on the harbour love,
And I wish I could remain,
For I know it will be some long time
Before I see you again.
(CHORUS)

Passenger's Luggage at Cobh, 1934.

Boys of Fairhill

A famous song from Cork which has the wonderful ability
to absorb new words about fresh events into the original fabric
of the song. New verses have been added gradually over the years.

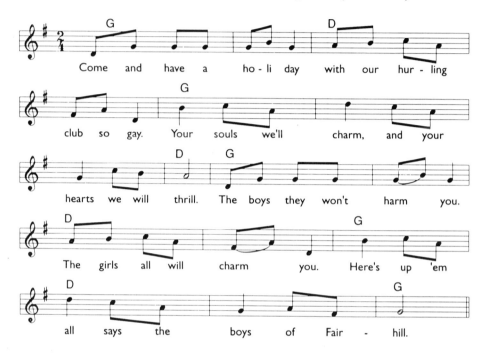

Come and have a ho - li day with our hur - ling
club so gay. Your souls we'll charm, and your
hearts we will thrill. The boys they won't harm you.
The girls all will charm you. Here's up 'em
all says the boys of Fair - hill.

Come on boys and you'll see, lads and lassies full of glee
Famous for all they will make your heart thrill.
The boys they won't harm you and the girls they will charm you
Here's up 'em all says The Boys of Fairhill,

Come on boys and spend a day with our Harrier Club so gay
The loft of the bowl it will make your heart thrill
When your hear the Shea boy say Timmy Delaney won today
Here's up 'em all says The Boys of Fairhill

Now come on up to Fahy's Well for a pint of pure spring water
The grandest place of all sure the angels do sing.
Thousands cross from o'er the foam
Just to kiss the Blarney Stone
Which can be viewed from the groves of Fairhill.

Come on down to Quinlan's pub, that is where you join our club
Where 'round us in gallons the porter does flow
First we'll tap the half a tierce
and drink a health to Dashwood's rule.
That's the stuff to give 'em says The Boys of Fairhill.

Now the stink on Patricks Bridge is wicked
How does Father Matthew stick it?
Here's up 'em all says The Boys of Fairhill.
Shandon Steeple stands up straight,
The river Lee flows underneath.
Here's up 'em all says the Boys of Fairhill.

Katty Barry sells crubeens, fairly bursting at the seams
Here's up 'em all says The Boys of Fairhill
Christy ring he hooked the ball
We hooked Christy, ball and all
Here's up 'em all says The Boys of Fairhill.

Blackpool girls are very rude, they go swimming in the nude
Here's up 'em all says The Boys of Fairhill
But then they are no good at all
Up against the Sunbeam wall
Here's up 'em all says The Boys of Fairhill.

The Juice of the Barley

A fine Limerick song in praise of whiskey.

Well when I was a gossoon of eight years or so,
With me turf and me primer to school I did go.
To a dusty old school house without any door,
Where lay the school master blind drunk on the floor.
(CHORUS)

14

At the learning I wasn't such a genius I'm thinking,
But I soon bet the master entirely at drinking,
Not a wake or a wedding for five miles around,
But myself in the corner was sure to be found.
(CHORUS)

One Sunday the priest read me out from the altar,
Saying you'll end up your days with your neck in a halter,
And you'll dance a fine jig between heaven and hell,
And his words they did frighten me the truth for to tell.
(CHORUS)

So the very next morning as the dawn it did break,
I went down to the vestry the pledge for to take,
And there in that room sat the priests in a bunch,
Round a big roaring fire drinking tumblers of punch.
(CHORUS)

From that day to this I have wandered alone,
A Jack of all trades aye and a master of none,
With the sky for my roof and the earth for my floor,
Sure I'll dance out my days drinking whiskey galore.
(CHORUS)

Shores of Amerikay

Emigration in the 19th century in Ireland was a major national disaster and a great source of inspiration for songmakers.

It's not for the want of employment I'm going;
It's not for the love of fame
That fortune bright may shine over me;
And give me a glorious name
It's not for the want of employment I'm going;
O'er the weary and stormy sea
But to seek a home for my own true-love;
On the shores of Amerikay.

And when I am bidding my last farewell;
The tears like rain will blind
To think of my friends in my own native land;
And the home I'm leaving behind
But if I'm to die on a foreign land;
And be buried so far away
No fond mother's tears will be shed o'er my grave;
On the shores of Amerikay.

Dun Laoghaire Harbour, Co. Dublin, 1929.

17

Sliabh na mBan

Charles J. Kickham, author of "Knocknagow", wrote these words
to an old tune "The Valley of Sliabh na mBan".

A - lone all a - lone___ by the wave washed strand___ all a - lone in a crowd - ed hall.___ The hall it is gay,___ and the waves they are grand,___ but my heart is not here at all.___ It flies far a - way___ by night and by day,___ to the time and the joys that are gone.___ And I ne - ver will for - get___ the sweet maid - en I met___ in the val - ley of Sliabh - na - mBan.___

18

It was not the grace of her queenly air;
Nor her cheek of the rose's glow
Nor her soft black eyes, nor her flowing hair;
Nor was it her lily white brow
'Twas the soul of truth and of melting ruth;
And the smile like a summer dawn
That stole my heart away on a soft summer day;
In the Valley near Sliabh na mBan.

In the festive hall, by the starwashed shore;
Ever my restless spirit cries
"My love, oh, my love, shall I ne'er see you more?
And, my land, will you never uprise?"
By night, and by day, I ever, ever pray;
While lonely my life flows on
To see our flag unfurled and my true-love to enfold;
In the Valley near Sliabh na mBan.

The Sun is Burning

Written by Ian Campbell, a well known Scottish folk singer,
telling us all about the Atomic bomb.

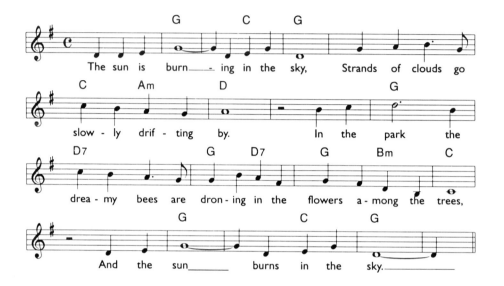

The sun is burn___ - ing in the sky, Strands of clouds go
slow - ly drif - ting by. In the park the
drea - my bees are dron - ing in the flowers a - mong the trees,
And the sun___ burns in the sky.___

Now the sun is in the West
Little babes lay down to take their rest,
And the couples in the park are holding hands
and waiting for the dark
And the sun is in the West,

Now the sun is sinking low.
Children playing know it's time to go.
High above a spot appears, a little blossom blooms
and then draws near.
And the sun is sinking low.

Now the sun has come to earth
Shrouded in a mushroom cloud of death.
Death comes in a blinding flash of hellish heat
and leaves a smear of ash
And the sun has come to earth.

Now the sun has disappeared
All that's left is darkness, pain and fear.
Twisted sightless wrecks of men go crawling on their knees
and cry in pain
And the sun has disappeared.

Fiddlers and Dancers at Emo, Co. Laois, 1936.

The Nightingale

This English song was made part of the repertoire of all Irish ballad
singers by Luke Kelly.

As I was a walk-ing one mor-ning in
May, I 'spied a young coup - le who fond-ly did
stray. And one was a pret-ty maid so sweet and so
fair, And the o-ther one was a sol-dier and a
bold gren-a-dier. And they kissed so sweet and
com-for-ting as they clung to each o-ther. They went
arm in arm a-long the road like sis-ter and
bro-ther. They went arm in arm a-long the road till they
came to a stream. And they both sat down to-
get-her for to hear the night-in-gale sing.

From out of his knapsack he took a fine fiddle
And he played such merry tunes as you ever did hear
And he played such merry tunes that the valley did ring
And they both sat down together to hear the nightingale sing

O soldier, O soldier will you marry me
O no, said the soldier, that never can be
For I have my own wife at home in my own counteree
And she is the sweetest little thing that you ever did see.

Now I'm off to India for seven long years
Drinking wines and strong whiskey instead of cool beers,
And if ever I return again it'll be in the spring
And we'll both sit down together and hear the nightingale sing.

Carndonagh Fair, Co. Donegal, 1929.

The Wearing of the Green

The author of that enduring play "The Recruiting Sergeant" wrote these words to a tune which has the same name but the words of which are concerned with the 1798 rebellion.

Oh Pad - dy dear and did you hear the news that's go - ing round? The sham - rock is by law for - bid to grow on Ir - ish ground. No more St. Pat - rick's Day we'll keep his col - our can't be seen. For there's a cru - el law a - gin the wear - ing of the green. I met with Nap - per - tan - dy and he took me by the hand, and he said "How's poor old Ire - land and how does she

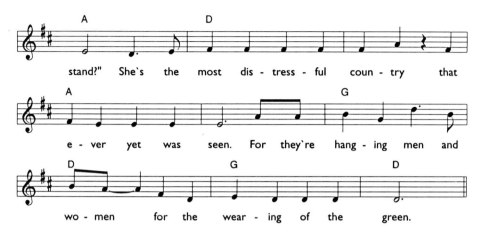

stand?" She's the most dis - tress - ful coun - try that e - ver yet was seen. For they're hang - ing men and wo - men for the wear - ing of the green.

And if the colour we must wear is England's cruel Red
Let it remind us of the blood that Ireland has shed.
Then pull the shamrock from your hat, and throw it on the sod
And never fear, 'twill take root there, tho' under foot 'tis trod.
When the law can stop the blades of grass from growing as they grow
And when the leaves in summertime, their colour dare not show
Then I will change the colour, too, I wear in my caubeen
But 'till that day, please God, I'll stick to wearing of the Green.

Slade Castle, Co. Wexford, 1930.

26

Bunch of Thyme

In this song, full of symbols, thyme is obviously virginity.
Several versions of this song exist both in Ireland and England.

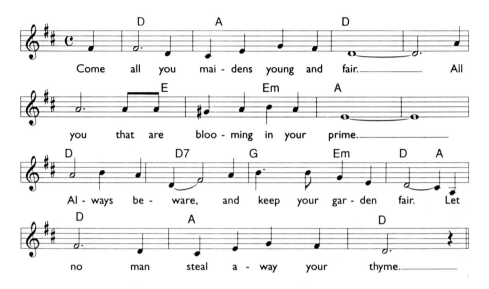

Come all you mai - dens young and fair. All
you that are bloo - ming in your prime.
Al - ways be - ware, and keep your gar - den fair. Let
no man steal a - way your thyme.

For thyme it is a precious thing
And thyme brings all things to my mind.
Thyme with all its pleasures along with all its joys.
Thyme brings all things to my mind.

Once I had a bunch of thyme
I thought it never would decay.
Then came a lusty sailor, who chanced to pass my way.
He stole my bunch of thyme away.

The sailor gave to me a rose.
A rose that never would decay.
He gave it to me to keep me in mind
Of when he stole my thyme away.
(Repeat first verse)

27

The Lark in the Morning

The theme recurs in folk songs. This version is from the North of
Ireland and is almost certainly of English origin. Cecil Sharp recorded
the same words to a different tune in England.

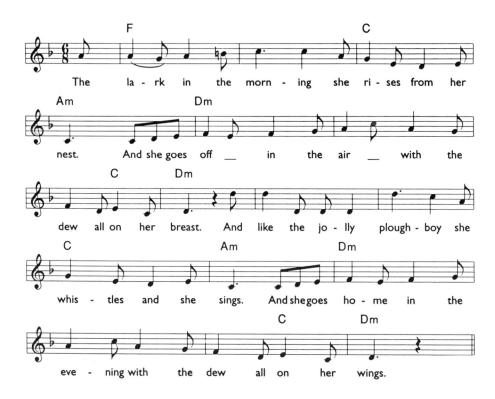

Oh, Roger the ploughboy he is a dashing blade,
He goes whistling and singing for yonder leafy shade
He met with dark-eyed Susan, she's handsome I declare,
And she is far more enticing than the birds all in the air.

As they were coming home from the rakes of the town,
The meadow bein' all mown and the grass had been cut down.
As they should chance to tumble all on the new-mown hay
Oh, it's kiss me now or never, this bonnie lass would say.

When twenty long weeks were over and past
Her mammy asked the reason why she thickened round the waist
'It was the pretty ploughboy' this girl then did say,
For he asked me for to tumble all on the new-mown hay.

Here's a health to you ploughboys where ever you may be,
That like to have a bonnie lass a sittin' on each knee.
With a pint of good strong porter he'll whistle and he'll sing
And the ploughboy is as happy as a prince or a king.

Donkey Tandem pulling logs, Mountmellick, Co. Laois, 1932.

Whiskey in the Jar

A song that has a version in almost every part of Ireland.
The idea of him getting aid from his brother
in the army is an intriguing one.

As I was go - ing o - ver, the
Kil - ma - gen - ny moun - tain, I met with Cap - tain
Far - rell and his mon - ey he was count - ing. I
first pro - duced my pis - tol and then I drew my
ra - pier, say - ing stand and de - li - ver for I
am a bold de - ceiv - er. With my Ring um - a doo - dle um - a
da whack fol di da - ddie - o
whack fol di da - ddie there's whis - key in the jar.

He counted out his money and it made a pretty penny
I put it in my pocket and I gave it to my Jenny
She sighed and she swore that she never would betray me
But the devil take the women for they never can be easy
(CHORUS)

I went into my chamber all for to take a slumber
I dreamt of gold and jewels and for sure it was no wonder
But Jenny drew my charges and she filled them up with water
And she sent for Captain Farrell to be ready for the slaughter.
(CHORUS)

And 'twas early in the morning before I rose to travel,
Up comes a band of footmen and likewise captain Farrell:
I then produced my pistol, for she stole away my rapier
But I couldn't shoot the water, so a prisoner I was taken.
(CHORUS)

And if anyone can aid me, it's my brother in the army
If I could learn his station in Cork or in Killarney
And if he'd come and join me, we'd go rovin in Kilkenny
I'll engage he'd treat me fairer than my darling sporting Jenny.
(CHORUS)

Buachaill ón Eirne

The narrator in this song has nothing but women on his mind.
It seems that nothing else in life matters to him and he advises
the rest of us in the strongest possible terms not to marry
an old grey headed person for obvious reasons.

Buacailleacht bó, mo leo, nár chleacht mise riamh.
ach ag imirt 's ag ól le hógmhná deasa fá shliabh.
Má chaill mé mo stór ní móide gur chaill mé mo chiall
Is ní mó liom do phóg ná an bhróg atá ar caitheamh le bliain.

Rachaidh mé amárach a dhéanamh leanna fán choill,
gan coite gan bád gan gráinín brach' ar bith liom,
ach duilliúir na gcraobh mar éide leapa os mo cheann.
Is óró, a sheacht m'anam déag thú, is tú ag féachaint orm anall.

A chuisle 's a stór ná pós an seanduine liath.
Ach pós an fear óg, mo leo, mura maire sé ach bliain
Nó beidh tú go fóill gan ó ná mac ós do chionn
A shilfeadh na deora tráthnóna nó'r maidin go trom.

"Shipping the Baby", Bantry, Co. Cork, 1930.

Grace

Joseph Mary Plunkett was one of the executed 1916 leaders. He was married on the eve of his death to Grace Gifford.

As we gat-her in the cha-pel here in old Kil-main-ham jail, I think a-bout the last few weeks oh will they say we've failed? From our school-days they have told us we must yearn for li-ber-ty, Yet all I want in this dark place is to have you here with me. Oh Grace just hold me in your arms, and let this mo-ment lin-ger. Then take me out at dawn, and I will die. With all my love I place this wed-ding ring up-on your fin-ger, There won't be time to

share our love, for we must say good - bye.

Now I know it's hard for you, my love,
to ever understand
The love I bear for these brave men,
my love for this dear land,
But when Padraic called me to his side
down in the G.P.O.,
I had to leave my own sick bed
to him I had to go.
(CHORUS)

Now as the dawn is breaking,
my heart is breaking too,
on this May morn as I walk out,
my thoughts will be of you,
and I'll write some words upon the walls,
so everyone will know,
I loved you so much that I could see
his blood upon the rose.
(CHORUS)

If I was a Blackbird

This song is closely associated with that great ballad singer of the fifties, Delia Murphy.

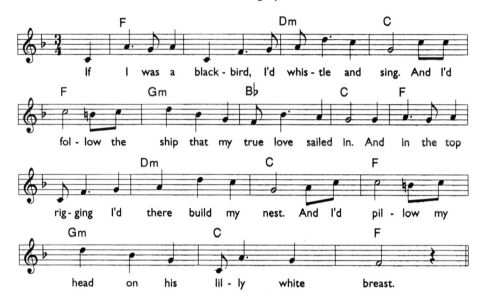

If I was a black-bird, I'd whis-tle and sing. And I'd fol-low the ship that my true love sailed in. And in the top rig-ging I'd there build my nest. And I'd pil-low my head on his lil-ly white breast.

I am a young maiden and my story is sad
For once I was courted by a brave sailor lad.
He courted me strongly by night and by day,
But now my dear sailor is gone far away.

He promised to take me to Donnybrook Fair,
To buy me red ribbons to tie up my hair.
And when he'd return from the ocean so wide,
He'd take me and make me his own loving bride.

His parents they slight me and will not agree
That I and my sailor boy married should be.
But when he comes home I will greet him with joy
And I'll take to my bosom my dear sailor boy.

Emigrant's Farewell, Cobh, 1934.

The Dear Little Shamrock

There's a dear lit-tle plant that grows in our Isle. 'Twas St. Pat-rick him-self sure that set it. And the sun on his la-bour with plea-sure did smile, And with dew from his eye of-ten wet it. It shines thro' the bog thro' the brake and the mire-land, And he called it the dear lit-le Sham-rock of Ire-land. The dear lit-le Sham-rock, The sweet lit-le Sham-rock, The dear lit-le sweet lit-le Sham-rock of Ire-land.

That dear little plant still grows in our land.
Fresh and fair as the daughters of Erin
Whose smiles can bewitch and whose eyes can command
In each climate they ever appear in.
For they shine through the bog,
Through the brake, through the mireland.
Just like their own dear little shamrock.
(CHORUS)

That dear little shamrock that springs from our soil
When its three little leaves are extended,
Denotes from the stalk we together should toil
And ourselves by ourselves be befriended.
And still through the bog,
through the brake, through the mireland
From one root should branch,
Like the shamrock of Ireland.
(CHORUS)

The Ould Triangle

Brendan Behan used this song to punctuate his play "The Quare Fella". A 'screw' is a prison warder and a 'lag' a long term prisoner.

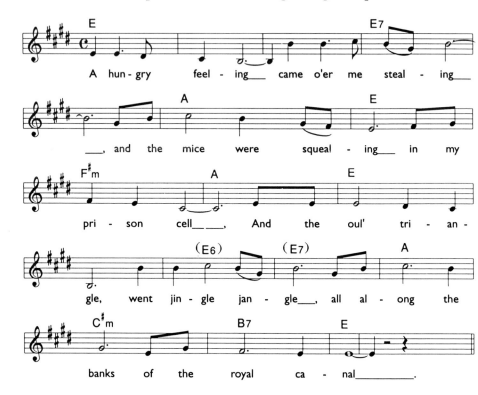

A hun-gry feel-ing___ came o'er me steal-ing___, and the mice were squeal-ing___ in my pri-son cell___, And the oul' tri-an-gle, went jin-gle jan-gle___, all al-ong the banks of the royal ca-nal___.

To begin the morning, the warder's bawling:
"Get out of bed and clean up your cell"
And that ould triangle went jingle jangle,
Along the banks of the Royal canal.

On a fine spring evening, the lag lay dreaming,
The seagulls wheeling high above the wall,
And the ould triangle went jingle jangle
Along the banks of the Royal Canal.

The screw was peeping, the lag was sleeping,
While he lay weeping for his girl Sal,
And the ould triangle went jingle jangle
Along the banks of the Royal Canal.

The wind was rising and the day declining,
As I lay pining in my prison cell
And the ould triangle went jingle jangle
Along the banks of the Royal Canal.

In the female prison there are seventy women
I wish it was with them that I did dwell,
Then that ould triangle could jingle jangle
Along the banks of the Royal Canal.

The day was dying and the wind was sighing
As I lay crying in my prison cell
And the ould triangle went jingle jangle
Along the banks of the Royal Canal.

A Place in the Choir

A bright lively children's song from America
made popular by Clancy & Makem.

The dogs and the cats they take up the middle,
Where the honey bee hums and the cricket fiddles,
The donkey brays and the pony neighs.
And the old grey badger sighs.
(CHORUS)

Listen to the top with the little birds singing
And the melodies and the high notes ringing,
And the hoot-owls cries over everything
And the blackbird disagrees.
Singing in the night-time, singing in the day,
And the little duck quacks and he's on his way,
And the other hasn't got much to say,
And the porcupine talks to himself.
(CHORUS)

It's a simple song, a little one sung everywhere
By the ox and the fox and the grizzly bear.
The dopey alligator and the hawk above.
The sly old weasel and the turtle-dove.
(CHORUS)

"The Gossips", Bantry, Co. Cork, 1930.

43

Queen of Connemara

A 'hooker' is a type of fishing boat with sails which is peculiar to
Galway. This one is obviously much loved by her skipper and
Frank Fahy that great Irish songwriter captures the romance
of a man, a boat and the sea in this joyful song.

Oh my boat can safe - ly float in the
teeth of wind and wea - ther, and out - race the fast - est
hook - er be tween Gal - way and Kin - sale, When the
black floor of the o - cean and the white foam rush to
geth - er, High she rides in her pride like a
sea - gull through the gale, Oh she's neat. Oh she's
sweet___, She's a beaut' in ev - ery line_____, The

Queen of Con - ne - mar - a is___ that bound - ing bark of mine.

When she's loaded down with fish,
'Till the water laps the gunwale,
Not a drop she'll take aboard her
That would wash a fly away;
From the fleet she speeds out quickly
Like her greyhound from her kennel,
'Till she lands her silvery store the first
On old Kinvara Quay.
(CHORUS)

There's a light shines out afar
And it keeps me from dismaying
When the clouds are ink above us,
And the sea runs white with foam,
In a cot in Connemara
There's a wife and wee ones praying
To the One Who walked the waters once
To bring us safely home.
(CHORUS)

The Good Ship Kangaroo

Elizabeth Cronin from Macroom in Co. Cork is the source
of this song made popular by Christy Moore.

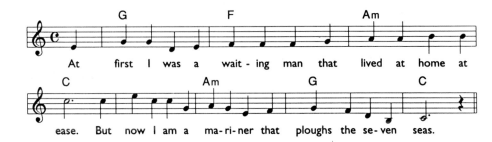

At first I was a wait-ing man that lived at home at ease. But now I am a ma-ri-ner that ploughs the se-ven seas.

I always loved seafarin' life, I bid my love adieu.
I shipped as steward and cook, me boys, on board the Kangaroo.

Chorus:
Oh I never thought she would prove false or either prove untrue
As we sailed away through Milford Bay on board the Kangaroo.

'Think of me, oh think of me,' she mournfully did say,
'When you are in a foreign land and I am far away.
Take this lucky trupenny bit, it'll make you bear in mind
That lovin' trustin' faithful heart you left in tears behind.'

'Cheer up, cheer up, my own true love. Don't weep so bitterly.'
She sobbed, she sighed, she choked, she cried
and could not say goodbye.
'I won't be gone for very long, 'tis but a month or two.
When I will return again of course I'll visit you.'

Our ship it was homeward bound from many's the foreign shore
And many's the foreign present unto me love I bore.
I brought tortoises from Tenerife and toys from Timbuktu
A china rat, a Bengal cat and a Bombay cockatoo.

Paid off I sought her dwellin' on a street above the town
Where an ancient dame upon the line was hangin' out her gown.
'Where is me love?' 'She's vanished, sir, six months ago
With a smart young man that drives the van for Chaplin,
Son and Co.'

Here's a health to dreams of married life, to soap suds and blue,
Heart's true love and patent starch and washin' soda too.
I'll go unto some foreign shore, no longer can I stay
And with some China hottentot I'll throw meself away

Me love she is no foolish girl, her age it is two score
Me love she is no spinster, she's been married twice before.
I cannot say it was her wealth that stole me heart away;
She's a washer in a laundry for one and nine a day.

"Climbing the Sign post", Balrothery, Co. Dublin, 1925.

The Patriot Game

In the fifties two young men from the Republic, Fergus O'Hanlon and
Seán South were killed in an attack on an R.U.C. barracks in Northern
Ireland. This song, by Dominic Behan, is O'Hanlon's song.

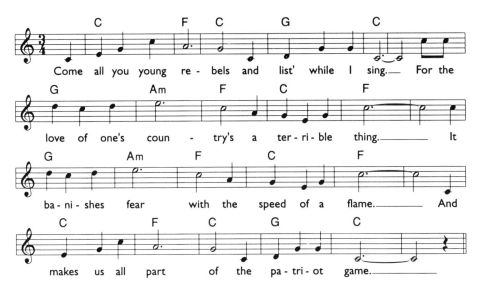

Come all you young re - bels and list' while I sing.— For the
love of one's coun - try's a ter - ri - ble thing.— It
ba - ni - shes fear with the speed of a flame.— And
makes us all part of the pa - tri - ot game.—

My name is O'Hanlon and I've just turned sixteen.
My home is in Monaghan where I was weaned.
I've learned all my life cruel England's to blame,
So now I am part of the Patriot game.

It's nearly two years since I wandered away.
With the local battalion of the bold I.R.A.
For I read of those heroes and wanted the same.
To play my part in the Patriot Game.

Now as I lie here, my body all holes.
I think of those traitors who bargained and sold.
I wish that my rifle had given the same,
To those quislings who sold out the Patriot Game.

Siúil a Ghrá

Many men went from Ireland with the 'flight of the Wild Geese'
and enlisted in French regiments. The missing lover in the song
joined the Irish Brigade which fought at Fontenoy.

His hair was black his eye was blue. His
arm was stout his word was true. I wish in my heart I
was with you. Go dté tú mo mhúir - nín slán.

Chorus
Siúil siúil siúil a ghrá; on - ly death can
ease my woe. Since the lad of my heart from
me did go; Go dté tú mo mhúir - nín slán.

50

I would I were on yonder hill,
'Tis there I'd sit and cry my fill,
And every tear would turn a mill,
Is go dté tú mo mhúirnín slán.
(CHORUS)

I'll sell my rod;, I'll sell my reel,
I'll sell my only spinning-wheel,
To buy for my love a sword of steel,
Is go dté tú mo mhúirnín slán.
(CHORUS)

I'll dye my petticoats, I'll dye them red,
And round the world I'll beg my bread,
Until my parents shall wish me dead,
Is go dté tú mo mhúirnín slán.
(CHORUS)

I wish, I wish, I wish in vain,
I wish I had my heart again,
And vainly think I'd not complain,
Is go dté tú mo mhúirnín slán.
(CHORUS)

But no my love has gone to France,
To try his fortune to advance,
If he e'er come back, 'tis but a chance,
Is go dté tú mo mhúirnín slán.
(CHORUS)

Will You Go Lassie Go

Frank McPeake recorded this song in 1957 for the series
"As I Roved Out" on BBC. He learned it from his uncle which gives it
definite Ulster credentials. "The Braes of Balquihidder" a song by the
poet David Taunahill from Perthshire in Scotland may be the origin of
the McPeake song.

I will build my love a tower
Near yon pure crystal fountain
And on it I will pile all the flowers of the mountain
Will ye go lassie go?
(CHORUS)

If my true love she were gone
I would surely find another
Where wild mountain thyme
Grows around the blooming heather.
Will ye go lassie go?
(CHORUS)

Old Style Cloak, Bantry, Co. Cork, 1930.

Crúiscín Lán

"The Brimming Jug" another lively song praising the pleasures
of alcohol. "Grá mo chroí" in Irish roughly means "heart's delight."

54

Immortal and divine great Bacchus god of wine
Create me by adoption your own son
In hope that you'll comply that my glass should never run dry
Nor my smiling little crúiscín lán lán lán
Oh my charming little crúiscín lán.
(CHORUS)

And when grim death appears in a few but pleasant years
To tell me that my glass it has run dry
I'll say begone you knave for bold Bacchus gave me leave
For to take another crúiscín lán lán lán
Oh my charming little crúiscín lán.
(CHORUS)

Regatta at Ballydavid, Co. Kerry, 1932.

55

I am a Little Beggarman

The words of this song were sold in broadsheet form possibly by the
song-maker who wrote it. This was common practice before the second
world war. The tune was collected in Dublin by Colm ó Lochlainn
in the twenties.

do.　　But　　run a-round　　the　　cor - ner with　his　 old rig - a - do.

I slept last night
In a barn at Currabawn.
A wet night came on
And I slipped through the door.
Holes in me shoes
And the toes peepin' through
Singin' skiddy-me-re-doodlum
For ould Johnnie Dhu.
(CHORUS)

I must be gettin' home
For it's gettin' late at night.
The fire's all raked
And there isn't any light
And now you've heard me story
Of the old ricadoo.
It's good-night and God bless you
From ould Johnnie Dhu.
(CHORUS)

The Meeting of the Waters

The old air "the Meeting of the Waters" obviously inspired the Thomas
Moore to write these words about that beautiful spot in Avoca, Co.
Wicklow. He called the song "There is not in this Wide World" but time
and public opinion have reclaimed the name of the original air.

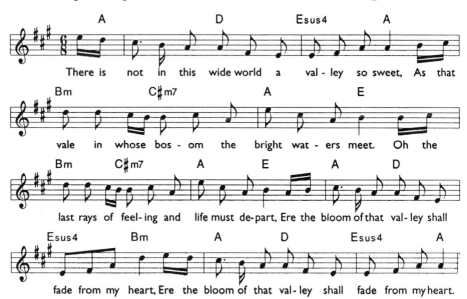

There is not in this wide world a val - ley so sweet, As that
vale in whose bos - om the bright wat - ers meet. Oh the
last rays of feel- ing and life must de-part, Ere the bloom of that val- ley shall
fade from my heart, Ere the bloom of that val- ley shall fade from my heart.

Yet it was not that nature had shed o'er the scene
Her purest of crystal and brightest of green
Twas not her soft magic of streamlet or hill
Oh! no it was something more exquisite still.

'Twas that friends, the beloved of my bosom, were near
Who made every dear scene of enchantment more dear
And who felt how the best charms of Nature improve
When we see them reflected from looks that we love.

Sweet Vale of Avoca! how calm could I rest
In thy bosom of shade, with the friends I love best
Where the storms that we feel in this cold world should cease
And our hearts, like thy waters, be mingled in peace.

Mackerel-fishing at Deepwater Quay, Cobh, 1934.

In Dublin's Fair City

The anthem of Dubliners was written by James Yorkston.

She was a fishmonger; But sure 'twas no wonder
And so were her father and mother before;
And they both wheeled their barrow
Through streets broad and narrow;
Crying cockles and mussels, alive, alive, oh!
(CHORUS)

She died of a fever; And no one could save her
And that was the end of sweet Mollie Malone;
But her ghost wheels her barrow
Through street broad and narrow;
Crying cockles and mussels, alive, alive, oh!
(CHORUS)

Children in front of the Magdalen Tower, Drogheda, 1925.

The Well Below the Valley

Collected in Boyle, Co. Roscommon this song is a good example of an
English song which has survived in Ireland but is now unknown in
England. It is a version of "The woman and the Palmer", based on the
story of Jesus and the woman of Samaria.

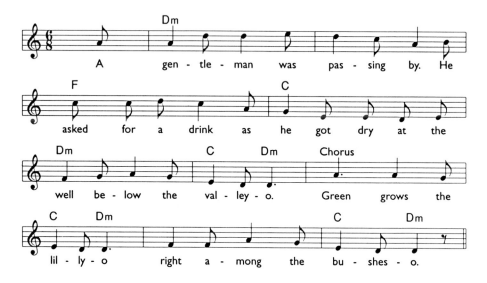

'Me cup is full up to the brim.
If I were to stoop
I might fall in.'
(CHORUS)

If your true love was passing by
You'd fill him a drink as he got dry
At the well below the valley-o.'
(CHORUS)

She swore by grass, she swore by corn,
That her true love had never been born
At the well below the valley-o.
(CHORUS)

He said, 'Young maid, your swearing wrong,
For six fine children you had born
At the well below the valley-o '
(CHORUS)

'If you be a man of noble fame,
You'll tell to me the father of them
At the well below the valley-o.'
(CHORUS)

'There's two of them by your Uncle Dan
At the well below the valley-o '
(CHORUS)

'Another two by your brother John
At the well below the valley-o '
(CHORUS)

'Another two by your father dear
At the well below the valley-o.'
(CHORUS)

'If you be a man of noble esteem,
You'll tell to me what did happen to them
At the well below the valley-o.'
(CHORUS)

'There's two buried 'neath the stable door
At the well below the valley-o.'
(CHORUS)

'Another two near the kitchen door
At the well below the valley-o.'
(CHORUS)

'Another two buried beneath the well
At the well below the valley-o.'
(CHORUS)

'If you be a son of noble fame,
You tell to me what'll happen meself
At the well below the valley-o '
(CHORUS)

'You'll be seven years a-ringing the bell
At the well below the valley-o '
(CHORUS)

'You'll be seven more a-burning in hell
At the well below the valley-o.'
(CHORUS)

I'll be seven years a ringing the bell
But the lord above me save me soul
From burning in hell
At the well below the valley-o '
(CHORUS)